From the Heart of the Florida Keys

Postcards from the Refuge
A Journey Through the National Key Deer Refuge

Carol Morrison   Nancy Chatelaine

Home of the Endangered Key Deer

Postcards from the Refuge
A Journey Through The National Key Deer Refuge

Carol Morrison
Nancy Chatelaine

Written by Carol Morrison, designed and illustrated by Nancy Chatelaine

© Copyright 2014 by Carol Morrison and Nancy Chatelaine for Palm Frond Press. All rights reserved. No part of this book may be reproduced, stored or transmitted in any manner whatsoever without prior written permission. All information in this book is accurate to the best of our knowledge. The authors, publisher and the National Key Deer Refuge disclaim any liability connected to details within this book.

Published by Palm Frond Press, Big Pine Key, Florida
palmfrondpress@earthlink.net
Printed in the U. S. A.

Dedication

This book is dedicated to all those whose early efforts brought wildlife refuges to the Florida Keys, and then maintained them over the years. While we cannot possibly name all those whose work was instrumental, we can cite some who are iconic for the National Key Deer Refuge: Jack Watson, the first Refuge Manager and the man who saved the Key deer; Frederick Mannillo, volunteer, who devoted his too-short life to the refuge; Mick Putney, a leader in energy conservation and wildlife preservation; and Harold and Susan Nugent, who just about everyone remembers as the wildlife godparents of today's refuge workers and volunteers.

Acknowledgments

We want to thank the refuge staff and volunteers for sharing their incredible expertise in the compilation of this book. We thank Anne Morkill, previous Florida Keys National Wildlife Refuges Manager, who supported this venture from its inception and throughout the entire publication process; Tom Wilmers, Wildlife Biologist, who knows more about birds than birds themselves; Jim Bell, Refuge Ranger, who laid out for us the pine rockland ecosystem, and Chad Anderson, Refuge Biologist, whose enthusiasm for this project nearly matched our own. Alison Higgins shared her knowledge of indigenous snakes and exotic predator snakes and the campaign to keep constrictor snakes out of the Keys.

Volunteers are intrinsic to the success of the Key Deer Refuge. We thank Leon Elder and other volunteers for demonstrating, both through interview and by example, the role of volunteers in the continuing success of the refuge.

Finally, we thank our husbands, George and Richie, for their continued support of our work.

Contents

The Wildlife Refuges of the Florida Keys vi
Foreword: A Journey Through the Refuges ix

Exploring the Habitats
Overview of the Habitats 3
Pine Rocklands 4
Inside the Hardwood Hammocks 5
Marshes, Solution Holes, and Transitional Wetlands 7
Mangrove Shoreline 9
Sand Beaches 10
Prescribed Fires: An Inconvenient Truth 14
Wildflowers: Tiny Treasures 17

Beginning A Refuge

Indiana Jones and the Wildlife Refuge 21
Jack Watson: The Man Who Saved the Key Deer 21
From Columbus to Fontaneda 21
A Boy Scout's Honor 22
Key Deer: A Keystone Species 25
Killing with Kindness 26
Bambi Doesn't Live Here 29

Understanding The Refuge
The Blue Hole: From Eyesore to Wildlife Haven 35
A Snake in the Grass 37
Alligators and Crocodiles 38
Where have all the Butterflies Gone? 43
Endangered Marsh Rabbits 45
Keys Raccoons 47
Birds in the Bush 49

Protecting The Refuge
Invasive Exotics: Intruders In Paradise 61

Defending The Refuge
Volunteers Matter 71
How You Can Help 72
Afterword 73

Postcards from the Refuge

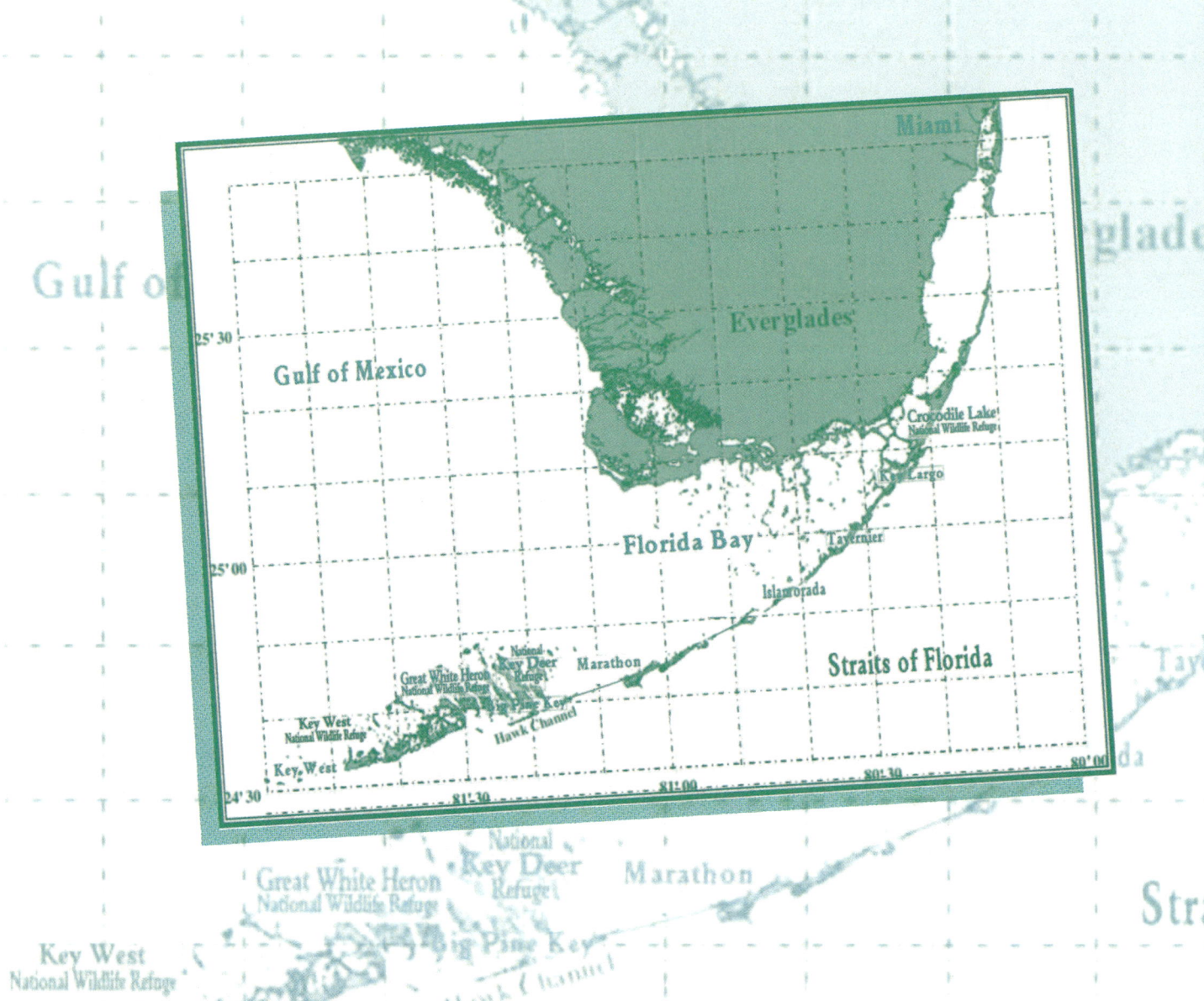

The Wildlife Refuges of the Florida Keys

There are four refuges within the Florida Keys National Wildlife Refuge complex: Crocodile Lake at the north, Key West at the south, Great White Heron and the National Key Deer Refuge centered on Big Pine Key. When we began this venture, our intention was to limit our subject to a manageable size by focusing only on the Key Deer Refuge. However, we soon discovered that many species, especially birds and butterflies, move freely from one refuge area to another, and are impossible to sort neatly into a single location. Therefore, we touch on the four interconnected refuges, but concentrate primarily on the National Key Deer Refuge on Big Pine and No Name Keys and refuge-owned outer islands. Since the four refuges are managed by the same administrators, their stories are both similar and different. They are similar in that they face some of the same challenges, but different in the species that are affected. This book covers most of the similarities, but what about the differences? Maybe that's another book.

This is not a research book. It is a *search* book. With the exception of some basic historical data and statistics from refuge bulletins housed in the refuge office, the information in these pages was gathered over several months of interviews with persons connected to the refuge. Professionals and volunteers work together to save and sustain the many species of plants and animals within the refuge. In reading this book, you will travel a journey much like our own, as we, the authors, searched for information and answers. Ultimately, you will be invited to join us in preserving a wildlife ecosystem unique in the world.

Postcards from the Refuge is a guide to the natural beauty and diversity of species within the Florida Keys wildlife refuges. It is more than just that, however: Beyond the scope of a visitors' guide, it also delves into the work of refuge staff, volunteers and local residents, as they combine efforts to maintain the Keys' ecosystem. Nature is always in flux, and it is the job of the refuge to protect species and habitats when they are challenged by natural or manmade threats. The complexity of that effort and the active cooperation of refuge staff and volunteers is part of the *Postcards* story.

"It was my first trip to the Keys and by the time we reached the boyos and the toy deer, I was completely surfeited with extraordinary and unheard-of natural wonders. Many of them were difficult to believe. It was possible to accept the region as subtropical, but the improbable combination of crocodiles, pink spoonbills, pirate gold, rock beauties, butterfly fish, panthers — and now toy deer — seemed like too much to swallow in one day. After all, this was Florida, USA, not the Great Barrier Reef on the other side of the globe. Or Africa, the land of the Golden Fleece."

Robert P. Allen,
from Natural History Magazine, February 1951,
recalling his first trip to the Florida Keys decades earlier.

Foreword
A Journey Through The Refuges

Florida's history is rich with accounts written by awed visitors to the Keys. From Fontaneda to Audubon to Robert Allen, each personal account reflects the thrill of discovering the plants and animals of what are now the Florida Keys National Wildlife Refuges. When we first came to the Keys, we followed in the footsteps of those who came before us, as we journeyed into the unique ecosystem. Like ours, your journey may take years, or like thousands of visitors each year, your journey may last only days. Regardless of the length and depth of your acquaintance with the refuges, this book will help you chart a course through the wonders waiting for you. You may travel by foot, bike, boat, car, or a combination of all four; but regardless of how you explore the refuges, you will benefit from firsthand information from the men and women who know the refuges best. We have searched out for you the people and places that will enable you to make the most of your time and journey.

Exploring The Habitats

Overview Of The Habitats

Pine Rocklands ◆ Inside the Hardwood Hammocks

Freshwater Marshes, Solution Holes, and Transitional Wetlands

Saltwater Marshes ◆ Mangrove Shorelines

Sand Beaches ◆ Prescribed Fires

Wildflowers

Postcards from the Refuge

Overview of the Habitats

As Florida naturalist Robert Allen observed in the enthusiastic description of his first trip to the Keys, there is a vastly greater range of plants and animals here in this small area than almost any place else in the world. How can this be? Quite simply, it is because of the various natural habitats found here and the relatively late intrusion of "modern" man. Here on Big Pine Key, the heart of the National Key Deer Refuge, this island alone supports more habitats attractive to diverse plant and animal life than anywhere else in the Keys or most other coastal areas of comparable size. Habitats range from hardwood hammocks to saltwater marshes, with scores of threatened and endangered wildlife supported within them.

In order to appreciate the many species of wildlife, both plant and animal, that exist within the boundaries of the National Key Deer Refuge, it is necessary, first, to understand the diverse habitats, and then which plants and animals live within them. In many cases, and for many reasons, the delicate balance of habitats and wildlife is currently threatened, and unless we act soon, some species may be lost forever.

Postcards from the Refuge

Pine Rocklands

When we began searching for interviews to write this book, we soon learned that we live in a rare ecological area. The pine rockland that covers much of Big Pine is distinct from most of the other keys.

Why Is Pine Rockland So Noteworthy?

Big Pine habitats can take many forms, from bushy and dense, thickly wooded areas; to prairie-like meadows; to barren, near-desert terrain; and marsh wetlands. Here on Big Pine, we have all of these, all in close proximity to one another. A walk

down a single trail can take you through samples of most of the habitats found on Big Pine. Barren caprock gives way to meadows, which give way to twisted thickets of brush, which give way again to pine and thatch palm rocklands with freshwater solution holes, which give way to mangrove marshes at the water's edge.

The one thing that all pine rocklands have in common is, of course, pines. Tall slash pines rise above the rocklands, with thatch palms, silver palms and weedy shrubs growing underneath. On the ground, various grasses and wildflowers spring up alongside seedlings from the trees. In other areas, the pines are scarce and there is no medium that can support much growth. Instead, there are vast expanses of oolite, a caprock that looks almost like pavement. In some back road areas, it *is* the pavement!

The fragility of the pine rocklands has prompted state and federal agencies to prohibit the removal of native plants. Indeed, many species are found only on Big Pine and only within the National Key Deer Refuge. This step is necessary in order to prevent extinction of species and to preserve the natural habitat for future generations of wildlife.

Unfortunately for pineland habitats, they are very attractive to developers. They tend to be dry, and it is relatively easy to scrape away the shallow root systems of trees and plants within the habitat and replace them with roads and home sites. If the refuge had not been created, most of the area between Eden Pines Colony and the Pine Heights subdivision would now be overrun with housing. Even today, you can follow paths from either Eden Pines or Pine Heights to view the vast wasteland of what had begun to be the extension of Eden Pines Colony, including an ambitious extension of the Eden Pines canal system. Streets and square blocks had been scraped into the caprock, and sites had been marked for houses that, thankfully, never were built. Today, that area is owned by the refuge and serves as free range for deer and other species.

On Big Pine, refuge land encompasses several differing habitats that exist side-by-side, and within them, differing flora and fauna.

Inside the Hardwood Hammocks

The Flora

A hardwood hammock is crowned by a dense canopy of indigenous hardwood tress, with smaller trees and bushes growing inside the hammock. Beneath all that plant life is a ground cover of native grasses and seedlings.

As leaves fall and decompose, a layer of humus is produced, which provides nutrients to plants within the hammock. Even more important, the thick humus acts like a sponge to hold water for the roots of canopy plants during the dry season.

The Fauna

Hardwood hammocks shelter and feed dozens of species of mammals, birds, reptiles, and insects, some of which are threatened or endangered for the same reasons as the hardwood hammocks themselves. Raccoons and other small mammals depend on fruits within the hammock as their primary source of food. Migrating and resident birds feed upon the insects,

fruits and flowers. Invertebrates of the hammocks include tree snails, spiders, and land crabs, which also feed upon insects and plants within the hammock.

Hardwood Hammocks

Throughout the Keys—not including Big Pine, No Name, and islands owned by the refuge—there has been a serious decline of hardwood hammocks as a result of human development. However, because of the Key Deer Refuge, both Watson's Hammock and Cactus Hammock on Big Pine have remained largely intact, and new hammocks are forming in various spots around the island.

Marshes, Solution Holes and Transitional Wetlands

Freshwater Marshes & Solution Holes

The Keys ecosystem is always changing, although so slightly and over so long a period of time, that it is imperceptible to most of us. In geological time, the Keys have been part of a solid landmass, coral reefs under the ocean, and various stages in between, depending on global temperatures melting and reforming polar ice caps, and other factors. Recent scientific data warn us that climate change has accelerated so rapidly that land loss is indeed measurable and even predictable. The waters surrounding the Florida Keys rise each year and habitat is lost.

More than just a hole in the rock, this solution hole holds fresh water for plants and animals.

The picture is complex. At one time, the ecosystem was composed mostly of pine rocklands, marshes and mangroves. Development and climate change, however, have altered the composition of the area. Now, fresh and saltwater marshes are mixed with pinelands all across Big Pine. Freshwater marshes form when rainwater is trapped in low areas of caprock, where marshy plant life grows, creating a hospitable watering site for refuge wildlife. In other places, solution holes, depressions where caprock has eroded, expose a lens of fresh water, providing drinking water for wildlife. The rock surface develops deep holes that enlarge over time, some becoming the size of small ponds. Others are as small as a quarter. Because the oolite holds rain water and keeps it clean, solution holes are reliable sources of fresh water, even during the dry season. Of course, there is salt water at the bottom of the holes, but since fresh water is lighter than salt, it floats on top, allowing species that require fresh water to live on Big Pine. Most solution holes are connected underground, making it possible for small alligators as well as fish and other creatures to travel through the subterranean tunnels. Wise hikers

This large solution hole is a reliable source of fresh water even in the dry season.

Postcards from the Refuge

never stick a hand or foot into a solution hole! Likewise, even the pinelands themselves are maintained by the same underground freshwater lens, supporting root systems of trees and other plants.

Solution holes, and other freshwater wetlands, provide fresh water to wildlife, but plant-eating animals, *herbivores*, must venture out into the open pinelands for food. This fact, of course, complicates efforts to save endangered species: They don't stay put in one area.

Transitional Wetlands and Saltwater Marshes

Between the pinelands and the saw grass that leads into the shallows of the ocean, a transitional area eases the terrain from rockland to saltwater marsh. Pines give way to buttonwoods that twist themselves into sentinels of the march, as the land slopes gently to the sea. Buttonwoods are related to mangroves, so they are able to tolerate some salt. Tides may rise into the transitional wetland, but the land is never permanently underwater. Until recently, that is.

Nearest the water, in fact growing into the water, are plants and trees that have adapted to the presence of salt. Salt is toxic to most plants, including most within the refuge. However, some plants, most notably some of the mangroves, can take in salt water, extract the fresh water they need, and then excrete the salt onto the outer surfaces of their leaves. This coating of salt is visible to the careful observer.

With the rising ocean levels, islands are losing land each year. This fact, of course, affects wildlife within the ecosystem. Most of the marsh rabbits, for example, have been driven by loss of habitat to the northern end of Big Pine, which is largely marsh land. Because of its remote location and forbidding terrain, the rabbits are relatively safe during the day. At night, however, they must leave their safe zone in search of food and fresh water. Today, even that safe zone is threatened, largely due to man's encroachment and rising ocean levels into what formerly was marsh rabbit habitat.

Postcards from the Refuge

Mangrove Shoreline

Mangroves Make Islands

When visitors to the Keys learn about the ecosystem, they are intrigued to discover that mangroves themselves are creating land. Mangroves can grow where other trees cannot because, depending on their species, they either exclude or extrude salt. Put simply, red mangroves exclude salt, they filter it out when they take water in. Black and white mangroves extrude salt, and push it out through their leaves after taking water in. Since they grow where other trees cannot, their roots have no competition in attracting and holding sediment, which in turn makes land. It is a slow process, crawling along over centuries before any significant land mass is formed. A drive along US1 will show tiny islands in the making and already-established small islands growing larger because of their mangrove shorelines. Entry is prohibited on most of the mangrove islands in the backcountry, but a few are open to the public. The refuge visitor center can show you which islands are accessible and suggest areas to explore by kayak.

Mangroves are important for another reason: They drop their leaves year round. The decomposing leaves are the primary food for crabs, clams, and other small ocean creatures. In addition, mangrove roots maintain the shoreline, a natural tool in preventing loss of land. For this reason it is illegal to disturb or cut down a mangrove. The fine for doing so is high. But considering the important work they do, perhaps it isn't high enough!

Postcards from the Refuge

Besides regular visits by Key deer and other species, mangroves provide food and shelter to various species of wading and shore birds, some of them endangered. Some species build nests in the mangroves, others just fly in for a quick meal. Fish and shrimp, especially young ones, hide from predators in knarled mangrove roots. The mangroves are truly a nursery for new ocean life.

Mangroves have been designated a "species of great concern," because of the many threats to their continued existence. Some threats are natural, including hurricanes and storms; others are manmade, including encroaching development, and runoff from fertilizers and industry. The mangroves are,

of course, worth saving in themselves; but since they also nourish various forms of life at the bottom of the ecosystem, all life above them depends on their presence.

Sand Beaches

Big Pine's Own Long Beach

One of the refuge's best kept secrets is the Long Beach Nature Trail, on the ocean side of Big Pine, running from Big Pine Fishing Lodge to the end of the long beach promontory. As its name implies, this is a very long beach, although definitely not a swimming beach. A nature trail begins at the curve of Long Beach Road, where a sign indicates the entry spot. Like other signs throughout the refuge, the area is marked "prohibited" *except to hikers and sightseers*. The trail leads through caprock, solution holes and marshy areas to sand dunes, where it diverges in opposite directions. Both take you across the top of the dunes and along the water. The white sand trails are easily navigated, since they are regularly tended by volunteers. Signs along the way point out species of interest.

Long Beach is a perfect place to take a camera. In just one walk, you will see examples of most of the habitats on Big Pine: big gumbo limbos twist their rust-colored way along the path, buttonwoods show the way to the sea, mangroves continue to form islands, and scores of lovely shrubs, trees and wildflowers invite butterflies to rest on their branches. The brilliant colors of the butterflies are heightened by the various shades of green,

yellow, brown and black of the foliage. You may be fortunate enough to snap a photo of a butterfly resting on a wildflower.

Long Beach Trail also offers an opportunity to study closely two species of mangroves. Near the road, on caprock flats, black mangroves dot the area. Run your finger along the top of a leaf and see the salt that has been extruded by the tree. Closer to the ocean, salt tolerant red mangroves grow next to and into the water. Their roots collect sediment that over centuries may become islands. And of course, beyond all this natural beauty, the ocean stretches out to the horizon.

It is wise to stay on the trail. Between the trail and the ocean is a formidable array of ancient rocks, seaweed, tide pools and sand, teeming with tiny living creatures. While it is interesting to observe these creatures from the trail, it can be uncomfortable to try to walk among them. Sea grasses wash in with the tides, making attractive feeding and nesting areas for crabs, flies and other endemic wildlife, but when humans misstep in their midst, the result can be downright unpleasant. Volunteers regularly clean the beach of debris, but the seagrass remains, since it is a vital niche in the ecosystem; it is home to amphipods, miniature shrimp, that provide food for all manner of residential and migratory shorebirds.

Postcards from the Refuge

The sand is precious to several species of wildlife. Horseshoe crabs reproduce there, and more importantly, sea turtles. The beach along Long Beach Road is the sole area on Big Pine where the giant turtles come each year to nest. Each female turtle returns to the beach where she was hatched, to lay her own eggs, many years later. If she cannot access that beach, her eggs will spill into the ocean, where they will die. Therefore, it is imperative that further development be prohibited on nesting beaches. Save-a-Turtle, a south Florida volunteer organization supervised by the Florida Fish and Wildlife Commission, monitors the nests each year, guarding against predators and manmade obstacles, and checking each empty nest for a live baby turtle or two that didn't climb out with the rest. Some of these volunteers are homeowners on Long Beach Road, which makes this nesting area relatively safe for turtles. Other volunteers from the area sacrifice sleep to walk the beach, ensuring the safety and privacy of nesting females and, later, their newly-hatched babies. No outside intruder, either human or animal, is allowed on some beaches during nesting season.

Prescribed Fires: "An Inconvenient Truth"

In nature, wildfires occur with enough regularity to maintain the balance of the ecosystem. Fires are a natural cleansing system: They refresh and replenish sources of food and shelter for the many species of animals within the habitat. When man develops the area, however, wildfires are no longer an option. Man's presence disrupts the course of nature, even when houses are adjacent to, rather than inside, the refuge area. Prescribed fires on refuge land, conducted by trained experts, become the only means of saving the pinelands and the wildlife within them. Pine rocklands depend on fire.

Why Can't We Manage Pinelands Without Fire?

First, in terms of the Key deer, their browsing level is only three or four feet high. They rely on plants at or below that level to sustain them. True, some neighborhood deer have been conditioned to reach higher up for food. Some will even stand on their hind legs to grab a tasty hibiscus flower or some tender leaves from a homeowner's prized plumbago. In the pinelands, however, a refuge deer's food choices exist only between the ground and its browsing level.

Pine rocklands are the central habitat of the Key Deer Refuge. A freshwater lens, present throughout the island in solution holes, depressions created by rainwater in caprock fissures, and life within the pinelands is dependent on that freshwater lens. In nature, pines maintain the forest. Pine needles dry out on the ground and lead to fire. The pine trees themselves remain alive, protected by their bark. Small palms within the pineland offer an extra boost of diversity in the food supply, and the palms themselves regenerate from the ground upward,

14

Postcards from the Refuge

following a fire. Each year, the palms provide nutritious berries for deer and other animals of the habitat. Overcrowding by exotics and other invasive plants is eliminated by fire, and sun-loving plants can re-establish themselves once the canopy of exotics has burned away. Grasses and tender new plants begin to re-carpet the pineland caprock, and the area grows lush with renewed life. The food supply is greater and more diverse. Through the centuries, fire sustained the pine rocklands and provided habitats for an entire ecosystem. Today, pine rocklands are critically imperiled across the globe, but here on Big Pine we still have time to save those we have left, if we act now.

Fire roads help keep burn under control

Some ask, Why not wait for natural fires to occur?

There are several reasons why this is not an option.

- ♦ Natural fires are dangerous and destructive in a fragmented and modified landscape, where homes and businesses are interspersed with pinelands.
- ♦ Prescribed fires can be conducted when weather conditions are close to perfect: during a non-drought period when the humidity is high and the winds are low. Natural fires often occur when the land and air are dry and the winds are high.
- ♦ Prescribed fires are implemented by a combination of experts from various agencies, all working together. Here on Big Pine, prescribed fires are conducted and monitored by refuge personnel, the local forestry crew and the fire crew from the Everglades, where prescribed fires maintain the pinelands.

New growth after a burn provides tender shoots for wildlife

- ♦ Prescribed fires reduce the likelihood of a disaster due to fire: They eliminate the fuels that feed wildfires, kill humans and animals, and destroy property. They also reduce the likelihood of intense fires that occur when a dense covering of plants is allowed to form.
- ♦ Ideally, in a prescribed fire, animals are able to outrun the fire, and care is taken to see that they do. A natural fire can be a fast-moving inferno that can rapidly swallow most of the wildlife in a habitat.

In a perfect world, it would be convenient to avoid fires altogether, but in today's world, the need for controlled burns is an inconvenient truth.

Almost immediately after a prescribed fire, growth begins anew

Wild Flowers: Tiny Treasures

A walk along the nature trails and fire roads within the refuge reveals unexpected treasures. If you look closely, you will find wildflowers, some blooming in clear view along the trail, others hiding beneath larger foliage. These are not the large showy blossoms you may expect in a tropical garden, but, rather tiny bursts of color that attract butterflies and bees and continue the cycle of life.

Pisonia, stopper, black bead, acacia and other little blossoms make a brilliant showing.

Postcards from the Refuge

Beginning A Refuge

Indiana Jones and the Wildlife Refuge
Jack Watson: The Man Who Saved the Key Deer
From Columbus to Fontaneda ♦ A Boy Scout's Honor
Key Deer: A Keystone Species
The Deer That Shopped Winn-Dixie
Killing With Kindness
Lit Up for Christmas ♦ Breakfast of Champions
Bambi Doesn't Live Here
Why Key Deer Are Endangered

Postcards from the Refuge

Indiana Jones and the Wildlife Refuge

Jack Watson, the Man Who Saved the Key Deer

The history of the National Key Deer Refuge could easily become a script for another Indiana Jones movie. It has all the elements: a rugged, larger-than-life hero with a singular mission, danger on all sides, unique animals and humans, and a resolution where good triumphs and the hero wins.

From Columbus to Fontaneda

The historical path leading to the federal designation of the Key Deer Refuge began with the fourth voyage of Columbus, when one of his sailors reported sightings of tiny deer on the islands we now know as the Lower Keys. Their next appearance in the historical record came in the writings of a Spanish shipwreck survivor, Escalante Fontaneda, who lived with the Calusa Indians for seventeen years, and wrote about his adventure in 1575. His notes about tiny deer are augmented by ships' logs that mention Key deer as a food source.

For hundreds of years, the Key deer went virtually unnoticed by outsiders, until cartoonist J. N. "Ding" Darling published a drawing in 1934, intended to stir up public outrage at the near extinction of what he termed "the miniature deer." The drawing shows tiny deer being relentlessly driven into the sea by huge men with rifles. In the water, the deer are being beaten to death or wounded by men and killed by their dogs.

The situation begged for Indiana Jones.

"The Smallest Species of Deer in North America, Alone, Unguarded And On The Way Out!"

Public outrage ensued, but nothing much happened beyond the 1939 ban against the hunting of Key deer. Unfortunately, by that time the herd had been nearly eradicated, and poachers continued to hunt Key deer. Hunters from Key West regarded Big Pine as their private hunting ground.

A Boy Scout's Honor

Here, the story becomes poignant. In 1947, Gary Allen, an eleven-year-old Boy Scout, accompanied his father to the Florida Keys. He had heard his father's tales about the nearly extinct "toy" deer of the Lower Keys, and wanted to see them himself. He was so moved by their plight that he began a personal letter campaign, writing first to President Truman, then to President Eisenhower. He asked for land to be set aside to save the rapidly dwindling Key deer. This Boy Scout's campaign was eventually championed by the influential Boone and Crockett Club, a national organization dedicated to the preservation of hunting ethics and the conservation of wildlife.

The National Key Deer Refuge was established in 1957, but the threat of extinction still loomed. Poaching was rampant, and the Key deer continued to die. By 1950, only twenty-five to thirty deer were left, and poaching continued unabated. We can only assume that the killings continued and reduced even further the number of Key deer.

This desperate situation was the cue for Indiana Jones, in the guise of Jack Watson, to enter the picture.

According to his son, Ray Birdsong, PhD., Jack Watson joined the U. S. Fish and Wildlife Service in 1946, with a territory so large that it is hard to imagine today. He served Florida from the Tamiami Trail, through the Everglades, down through the Florida Keys and out to Dry Tortugas. He worked this territory alone, and soon made his presence felt, especially to poachers.

Jack Watson was a man for the times. His convictions were unwavering, his authority unquestioned and his methodology unique. He was a big man who used his size and his office as a one-man force to protect the Key deer. He scared off poachers, educated children about wildlife and garnered vast public support for the Key Deer Refuge. In 1973, he was named "Conservationist of the Year" by the National Wildlife Federation. When he retired in 1975, the Key deer herd had grown to 400.

Today, Jack Watson's name is very much alive on Big Pine. The only paved road that bisects the island is Watson Blvd. Like its namesake, it covers a lot of territory. Watson Blvd. begins at the gate of the refuge headquarters, runs across the island, makes a forty-five degree turn north, crosses a small bridge and ends at the big bridge to No Name Key. Children play baseball at Watson Field, and Keys visitors hike Watson Trail, where Jack Watson's educational outreach continues with posted descriptions and explanations about the flora and the fauna within the habitat.

Postcards from the Refuge

Key Deer: a Keystone Species

Who Holds the Key to Their Survival?

As a keystone species, the Key deer serve as a barometer of the health and vitality of the entire ecosystem. A *keystone species* is high in the food chain, and plays a crucial role in maintaining the balance of other species, both plant and animal. If the keystone species is harmed or removed, the species below it will suffer as well. Therefore, protecting the endangered Key deer is important not only for the survival of that particular species, but also for the survival of all wildlife within the refuge.

> *"As go the deer, so goes the refuge."*
> — JIM BELL, REFUGE RANGER

Refuge staff divide the Key deer into two categories: *refuge deer* and *neighborhood deer*. The refuge deer live on uninhabited islands or very remote parts of inhabited islands, including Big Pine and No Name, with smaller populations on other islands in the Lower Keys. They rarely come in contact with humans and maintain a healthy fear of us. Some suggest that since it is far safer and far healthier for deer to live on islands without human contact, we should just round them up, transport them to outlying islands, and convert the entire herd to refuge deer.

However, the deer have something to say about that idea. Deer choose where to live, and if transported off Big Pine, they simply swim back. In fact, since Big Pine has reliable access to fresh water, many does swim to uninhabited islands to give birth, tend to the fawns on the remote site, but swim back to Big Pine each day to drink from freshwater wetlands. From a deer's viewpoint, Big Pine and No Name Keys conveniently provide the basic needs for survival: fresh water, an ample food supply and shelter for themselves and their fawns.

Why, then, do some deer remain refuge deer and others become neighborhood deer? The location of their birth is probably the deciding factor. Deer tend to be highly territorial, covering and recovering the same area over and over again. If a fawn is born to a neighborhood doe, the fawn will also become a neighborhood deer. Indeed, the refuge has purchased large tracts of land within areas of human habitation, so the deer can move freely and live as normal a life as possible. A large percentage choose the easy lifestyle of the neighborhood deer. In fact, they become so tame that people give them names and treat them almost as pets. This is not a good thing.

Why? The human factor. Deer are docile and beautiful; and well-intentioned but uninformed people seem unable to resist contact with them. Allowing deer to beg for food can be regarded as a death sentence for the deer—and is a federal crime for the human.

The Deer That Shopped Winn-Dixie

A mature doe that locals named Dixie, lived in the woods surrounding the Winn-Dixie Shopping Center. She worked the parking lot each day, charming tourists who snapped endearing photos and rewarded her with tasty bits of food. Dixie even endured those who petted her back and rubbed her head. She was indeed a friendly little deer, but her real motivation in seeking human contact was the likelihood of an easy meal, not a desire to be a pet.

This habit very likely proved deadly. Dixie walked nonchalantly through the parking lot, with some cars dodging her and others stopping to look. She also criss-crossed Key Deer Blvd., knowing that a car would stop and people would give her food. Cars and deer are a deadly combination. When deer become tame as a result of mistaken kindness, i.e. feeding them from cars or alongside roads, their lifespan is cut short. Almost certainly, they will be killed by an unfortunate motorist.

Dixie has not been seen for a very long time.

A grim reminder of the lethal mix of cars and deer is a sign with the running tally of deer killed on the roads each year. Located just off U.S. 1, at the point where Key Deer Blvd. and Wilder Road diverge, the sign shows that a deer dies, on average, every three or four days. Since deer are not likely to learn to look both ways before crossing, it is up to those of us who share their habitat to watch for them when driving, and refrain from feeding them. Ever.

Killing with Kindness

A second reason not to feed deer is the likelihood of disease and intestinal blockage caused by the ingestion of foods not appropriate for consumption by deer. When deer gather to eat food provided by humans, their close proximity to one another risks infection of many deer, although only one may be ill initially. While feeding, other deer are exposed to diseases they would otherwise never encounter.

A little-understood illness has recently been found in Key deer: a virulent brain abscess that is always fatal. Can the infection be passed by one deer to others at a communal feeding area? That answer is unknown. However, it is known that, previously, only bucks were seen with the infection, most likely transmitted by open wounds incurred during their fights over females during mating season. Recently, however, does have been exhibiting the disease as well. Common sense indicates that artificially bringing deer together in a close feeding situation is likely to spread the deadly infection.

Another, even more prevalent killer, is an infection also transmitted by one deer to others through close feeding quarters. Necrobaciliosis, commonly called lumpy jaw, is highly contagious and untreatable. The deer always die. The jaws grow misshapen and out of alignment until, eventually, the deer is unable to chew.

Likewise, easy feeding allows weaker deer to survive and leads to overpopulation. When the herd gets too big, the food supply becomes inadequate, and even healthy deer starve to death. In northern states, deer herds are regularly thinned by allowing deer hunting in season. Here on Big Pine, however, such a solution would be impossible, even if it were acceptable—which it is not. It would be both dangerous and illegal to hunt and kill an endangered species that lives in family neighborhoods alongside humans.

Finally, replacing the deer's natural diet with unnatural foods causes malnutrition and even death. Some residents feed lettuce to the deer, thinking it resembles their natural food sources. It does not. Even worse, iceberg lettuce has almost no nutritional value. It makes the deer feel full but its food value is negligible. Other residents leave out cracked corn for the deer, again thinking it duplicates their natural food sources. Not true. Deer greedily eat the cracked corn—and in some cases, eat themselves to death. Literally. The corn clogs the deer's intestinal track, and the animal dies of infection and/or starvation.

Refuge land is abundant with natural sources of food. There is no need for humans to alter the balance. To do so can kill Key deer.

Lit Up for Christmas

Illegal feeding of deer can lead to unexpected outcomes. When deer root through the brush looking for food left out by humans, odd things happen. A magnificent buck with a heavy rack of antlers made a Christmas Eve visit to a beautifully decorated yard. As he rummaged, looking for free food, a string of Christmas lights became entangled in his antlers. The homeowner saw what happened and went to the rescue. The buck wanted the lights OFF, but was so spooked by the situation that he fled into the woods, leaving the homeowner behind with empty hands and good intentions. A few days later, the buck visited the yard of a home deep in the woods, where the homeowners were able to calm him and snip off the string of lights.

After the fact, some of us joked that we should have given the buck a battery pack to light him up as he moved through the refuge on Christmas Eve. In reality, though, the incident was serious, even deadly. If the string of lights had become tangled in heavy brush and vines, the buck would have been trapped there until he died of starvation. In this case, the homeowner with the Christmas lights had not fed the deer himself, but because others had, the deer rooted for food in a dangerous area.

The Breakfast of Champions

At various times of the day and season, Key deer can be found in various habitats, depending on their need for food, water, rest or shelter. During the hot daytime hours, Key deer tend to seek the shade of hardwood hammocks and pineland areas thick with brush. Between dusk and dawn, they come out to feed in more open areas. The refuge contains scores of plants the deer can and should eat. In the wild, deer are exclusively herbivores, that is, plant-eating animals. Unfortunately, the neighborhood deer have discovered garbage cans. The night before garbage pickup, the deer make a picnic of the contents of overturned garbage cans. Besides being annoying for the property owner, this practice is dangerous for the deer.

One morning, early-rising residents were surprised to see a young doe lurching down the street with a cereal box over her head, trying in vain to shake it off. No doubt she had been trying to reach a sweet-smelling bit of cereal at the bottom of the box, when her head became stuck. The box completely covered her eyes, and she soon would have been hit by a car or fallen into a canal, if no one had come upon the situation in time. Removing the box was easy, but it was another reminder that deer and humans don't belong together.

Unfortunately, deer have been conditioned to rummage through garbage cans, where all sorts of hazards hide. Rotting food. Insecticides. Sharp objects. Broken glass. A refuge biologist even saw deer eating the leftover bones of frog legs! Another saw deer dining on the remnants of the remaining crust *and* the box from a local pizzeria. Many Big Piners have learned that it is best not to set out garbage cans until morning. If that is not possible, they secure the lids with heavy bungee cords or use cans with locking lids. This practice makes things easier on the humans and safer for the deer.

Bambi Doesn't Live Here

As children, many of us saw the movie *Bambi* and vividly remember the heartache that followed the death of Bambi's mother. We remember Bambi as a frightened little fawn orphaned by a hunter's gun.

Perhaps that's why so many visitors—and even some residents—assume that any lone fawn they see must be an orphan. The first instinct of the kind-hearted human is to feed the fawn, which is exactly the wrong thing to do. It is likely that the fawn's mother is nearby, foraging for food. Like human mothers, does allow their babies more and more distance as they grow. You can usually be sure that the cute spotted fawn you see on the roadside or on someone's lawn has a mother closely watching, just beyond your line of vision. Can you imagine the terror for both the fawn and the doe if a well-meaning human grabs the fawn and puts it in a car? A refuge biologist was recently called by a person in a car, who was trying to force milk down a fawn's throat. The biologist, of course, asked where the fawn had been found, and returned it to the same location. Then he watched from a distance as the fawn called for its mother. Sure enough, she emerged from the brush and reclaimed her baby.

What should you do, then, if you find a fawn? Do nothing. At least for a reasonable length of time.

Stay far enough away from the fawn that its mother will not be afraid to come for it. When that happens, you will be treated to a small but memorable reunion. This is how nature works. But what should you do if a fawn remains alone too long? You may wonder whether the doe had been hit by a car—probably the only way Bambi would be orphaned on Big Pine. If she died, she would likely be on or near the road. Then you would call the refuge. Even if you find no evidence of a road kill, you should call the refuge if the fawn seems stressed or has been without its mother for too long a time. Under no circumstance should you touch the fawn, try to move it, or try to feed it. The fawn will not starve. Let the professionals from the refuge make the decision. In most cases they will try, first, to wait for the mother to return before taking any further action. If she does not come for the fawn, the refuge will handle the situation. They are trained wildlife specialists who know exactly what to do.

Why Key Deer Are Endangered

Since the Key deer herd has re-established itself so successfully over the last several years, some onlookers wonder why they continue to be classified as endangered. The answer is simple: Key deer will probably always remain on the endangered list because of their limited range. One natural catastrophe, such as a Category 4 hurricane, would decimate the entire herd. Experiments to establish small herds on other keys are showing some success, but for all practical purposes, the herd is concentrated on Big Pine and adjoining No Name Key. That's the way the deer want it.

So, then, back to the question that headed this chapter: Who holds the key to the survival of the Key deer? We all do.

Postcards from the Refuge

Understanding The Refuge

The Blue Hole: From Eyesore to Wildlife Haven

Alligators and Crocodiles ♦ Where Have the Butterflies Gone?

Endangered Marsh Rabbits ♦ Keys Raccoons

A Bird in the Bush ♦ A Snake in the Grass

Postcards from the Refuge

Greetings from the Blue Hole! Big Pine Key, FL USA

The Blue Hole

From Eyesore to Wildlife Haven

The Blue Hole began as a borrow pit, or rock quarry, dug out of caprock for the construction of highways on Big Pine. When the excavation hit sea water, the pit was abandoned and eventually filled with salt water. Over time, rainfall topped the sea water, creating the perfect environment for a year round panoply of wildlife. Because salt water is heavier than fresh water, a permanent lens of fresh water settled over the surface. Suddenly, an old borrow pit had a new look and a new purpose. The blue water and the plant life around the pond made it the perfect setting for man to observe more diverse wildlife in one setting than he would likely see in an entire afternoon trekking through the island. The refuge personnel saw in this unique location an opportunity to educate people firsthand. The Blue Hole, then, was named after the freshwater lens that made such a venture possible. Currently, the Blue Hole is visited by thousands of people each year. Signage and refuge volunteers aid visitors in spotting and photographing various species of animals, fish and plants that would otherwise escape their notice. A viewing platform allows visitors to safely watch the alligators, and a paved parking area with wheelchair access makes the Blue Hole an inclusive and safe destination. The natural beauty of the Blue Hole attracts both amateur and professional photographers, so take your camera!

To augment what they already had, the Blue Hole was stocked with turtles and fish. Some of the larger freshwater species of fish were imported from the mainland, so they are truly Florida fish, just not Keys fish. Freshwater fish endemic to the Keys are very small, which is true of many other species on Big Pine. But they all have a role in nature's design. The tiny gambusia fish, for example, have been a longtime weapon against mosquitoes, since they feed primarily on mosquito

Postcards from the Refuge

larvae. Even today, some of the shallow, manmade mosquito ditches continue to be stocked with gambusia, and mosquito control trucks invite homeowners with freshwater ponds to stock them with gambusia. Sometimes the old ways are still effective.

Unfortunately, non-native species have been released or dumped into and around the Blue Hole by irresponsible pet owners. Some of these fish and turtles are very showy and exotic, but they are actually dangerous to endemic species. They eat the native fish and disturb the ecosystem. In nature's plan, species have an important relationship: for example, a heron eats a baby alligator; and an adult alligator eats the heron.

Even very diverse species within the same ecosystem depend on one another for existence.

Some species live year round at the Blue Hole, but even more stop at the Blue Hole as a resting spot during their migrations. Animals instinctively search for fresh water, so each day is a new adventure at the Blue Hole. Who will be there today? Not only do birds and turtles visit the Blue Hole; Key deer, raccoons, iguanas, harmless snakes and various other species seek its fresh water as well.

Today, no one would call the Blue Hole an eyesore. It is the most popular attraction on Big Pine Key.

A Snake in the Grass

Not only are native snakes part of the refuge ecosystem, they are also benefactors for its human residents. Snakes play an important role in keeping lizards, toads, frogs and non-native pests within bounds, and help to reduce the numbers of invasive species breeding here. Three of the snake species are nonpoisonous and quite lovely. Some common species include black racers, rosy rat snakes and corn snakes. Their names tell some of their story: they eat rats and other vermin and help to maintain the balance of species within the ecosystem.

Big Pine's ringneck - a good, native snake

The only poisonous snake native to the refuge is the eastern diamondback rattlesnake. They were here long before man ventured down the Keys, staking out land. Early stories and written logs mention diamondbacks, and one eccentric settler is said to have sought land where rattlesnakes were present in order to deter trespassers.

Visitors to the refuge are unlikely to come upon a rattlesnake, but care should be taken when hiking in areas attractive to rattlesnakes: sunny rocky areas, mulch piles and heavy brush. They sometimes turn up in swimming pools as well. If you see a rattlesnake, keep your distance and call the refuge, if the snake is in a populated area. If the rattlesnake is in an unpopulated area, just leave the area and allow the snake to continue on its way.

If you are fortunate enough to come upon one of our nonpoisonous snakes, stand quietly and watch its movement. You may be surprised at its grace and beauty.

Postcards from the Refuge

"Grandmother, What Big Teeth You Have!"

Alligators and Crocodiles

Alligators seek the best food source and fresh water. Within the National Key Deer Refuge, the Blue Hole offers a continuing smorgasbord of foods preferred by American alligators. It also has a lens of fresh water, making it the perfect habitat. The Blue Hole is the only spot in the Keys where visitors can reliably view live alligators from the safety of a viewing platform.

All alligators are not equal. In general, the largest male claims the Blue Hole as his territory, where he reigns until he dies or loses a challenge from another male alligator. Of course, he allows at least one female to join him, sometimes more. Whenever another alligator tries to enter the Blue Hole, the resident male investigates, repelling smaller male alligators and juveniles, but allowing females to enter. On some occasions, when the male dies, his mate will remain in the Blue Hole until she accepts a male to join her.

Alligators mate each spring, usually in April or May. Very young or very old females don't bother to make a nest; they just lay their eggs in a secluded spot and watch over them. Mature females, however, dig a secure nest for their twenty to sixty eggs. After a two month incubation period, the eggs hatch and are aggressively guarded by the female. Hatchlings are eight to ten inches long, and grow up to one foot each year. Baby alligators are prey to migratory birds and other species, and few survive to reach adulthood. Their dark color, however, does help the baby alligators to camouflage themselves and, later, fool non-suspecting prey into thinking they are harmless logs floating in the water. Here, again, is an example of a cyclic relationship. Those surviving alligators themselves become predators as they grow, and eat as prey some of the same species that formerly hunted them. Alligators are vicious hunters, and with their wide mouth and huge teeth, they can attack and eat almost any prey smaller than they are. This explains why children and pets are more frequently attacked by alligators: their small size makes them vulnerable. The bigger the alligator, the bigger the prey. It also explains why alligators have not changed since they swam the waters of the world many millennia ago: Alligators are perfect killing machines, perfectly suited to their environment.

Both the drama and the cycle of life for alligators are visible over time at the Blue Hole. The same alligators live there for a period of years, until nature or predation by man leaves a void to be filled eventually by another dominant male and his mate(s). Then the cycle begins again.

The refuge provides a raised viewing platform, where visitors can observe the alligators and other species that inhabit the Blue Hole. Signs and printed material help visitors to see and appreciate the panorama before them. Often, a refuge volunteer is on hand to talk about the alligators and answer questions. To the visitors' delight, the alligators spend large amounts of time resting in the shallow water in front of the platform, hoping for handouts of food

A troubling side note to this story is man's invasive role, making humans the primary predator of alligators, even at the Blue Hole. Just as feeding key deer along the roadside leads to deer deaths, feeding alligators from the viewing platform leads to alligator deaths. Feeding alligators is dangerous: They learn to associate humans with food, thus increasing the likelihood of an alligator attacking humans or pets. Also, it conditions them to think that anything falling into the water near the platform is food; and it takes away the alligators' instinctive fear of man. As a result, people who absentmindedly eat food while viewing alligators may be issuing a dangerous invitation for an alligator to leave the water and take the food. Alligators move so fast that people would have little time to react. Likewise, people who walk their dogs close to the Blue Hole need to be aware of the alligator's rapid attack and gaping mouth. People who harass the alligators by dropping stones or plastics onto a resting alligator's  head—probably in an attempt to provoke movement from the alligator—not only may incite the alligator; they may induce the animal to eat the foreign objects. Sadly, feeding alligators accustoms them to the presence of humans and the connection of humans with food, making them easy prey to both intentional and unintentional deaths at the hands of humans. There are good reasons that food is illegal at the Blue Hole.

Appalling as it is, the Blue Hole has lost several alligators to deadly attacks by humans. Because the alligators are acclimated to the presence of humans, they lose their innate wariness and become easy targets for mean-spirited people. Alligators have been shot at close range, bludgeoned with baseball bats, even butchered for a barbeque. USFWS and law enforcement does not take these cruel transgressions lightly. Nor do local residents. Alligators are listed as threatened by federal regulation, and the unnecessary loss of even one alligator is not tolerated. The public vocally supports the arrest and trial of those who harm the alligators. These criminals are punished to the full extent of the laws protecting wildlife within the refuge.

Other alligators die as a result of objects dropped into the water, often by accident. Recently, Bacardi, a nine foot male alligator, was killed by a lethal obstruction in his digestive system. (Bacardi was named as a result of the number 151 on his FWS tag, which is the same as the alcohol content in overproof rum.) At the time of his death, Bacardi was seriously underweight and had no doubt suffered greatly for weeks. Alligators have very strong digestive juices—they can easily digest the bones of prey—but they cannot digest plastic. No living thing can. The necropsy showed several plastic objects blocking the movement of food. Bacardi had continued eating: remains of previous meals were still lodged at the point of the obstruction. No doubt that undigested food had contributed to the rampant bacterial infection that killed him. The actual objects found in Bacardi's stomach are on display at the refuge visitor center. One can easily see that, individually, these objects were not intended to be lethal; but when bunched together, they killed Bacardi.

Crocodiles in the refuge are more rare than alligators: They are classified as threatened by the federal government and, like the alligators, are absolutely protected from harassment or poachers. Crocodiles do inhabit the lower Florida Keys, but are rarely sighted by humans. Most live in the Key Largo area, where the Crocodile Lake National Wildlife Refuge is aptly named. Crocodiles within that refuge have rebounded so well that only their limitation to that habitat causes them to remain threatened. Like the Key deer, one large local catastrophe, such as a Category 4 hurricane, could decimate the entire population. Crocodiles can live in either salt or fresh water, and here in the Keys, they can be found in either habitat. On one occasion, a crocodile actually entered the Blue Hole, but stayed for only a week, no doubt chased out by the dominant alligator.

Crocodiles suffer from a popular misapprehension: Most people believe that crocodiles are man-eaters, probably due to television and films. While there are only two species of alligators—Chinese and American—there are twenty-three species of crocodiles. Only the Australian crocodiles, found in salt water, and the African crocodiles, found in fresh water, commonly view humans as prey. American crocodiles,  like American alligators, feed opportunistically on most living creatures unfortunate enough to cross their paths. Only rarely does that include man.

In general, crocodiles look like alligators but differ in significant ways: Their color is lighter and their snouts are narrower, and they look like they need a good orthodontist. Some of their teeth protrude from their mouths, probably making them look fiercer than they really are. Also, unlike alligators, crocodile mothers are not protective. When their young hatch, the mothers gather them into their mouths and deposit them in the water. From that point on, the hatchlings are on their own. They hide in weeds and other cover until they are big enough to survive among potential predators.

Where Have All the Butterflies Gone?

The Butterfly Bush Half Empty

Butterflies have always been plentiful on Big Pine. The already warm and pleasant winters are made even more colorful by the migrating birds and butterflies that stop here to intermingle with the native species. They flutter through the neighborhoods, sipping nectar from flowers and water from deeply veined leaves. They crisscross the sunny pinelands and seek shelter in cool hardwood hammocks. However, since they are most frequently found in the pinelands, it follows that changes to the habitat will affect the butterflies, and recent studies raise some troubling questions.

Today, one of the disconcerting mysteries faced by the refuge is where so many butterflies have gone, and why. Were they killed by Hurricane Wilma? That may seem to be an easy answer, but the fact is that butterflies were already declining before the hurricane. Did the butterflies migrate to other locations and re-colonize there? Are we looking in the wrong places? After all, it is impossible to look in all places at all times. One thing is certain, however: Butterfly populations are diminishing in the Florida Keys.

Butterflies are complicated. It is natural for an island ecosystem like Big Pine to experience waves and wanes of butterfly species. They may thrive in an area for years, then suddenly collapse in number. Where do they go? Will they reappear elsewhere? The answers to those questions are elusive. One thing is certain, however: As land is developed and the environment altered, there is less and less space for wildlife, and the potential for serious decline is real. It is extremely difficult to track butterflies, but a large-scale reduction in numbers is evident. As refuge biologist Chad Anderson observes, "They are ephemeral species. You can visit the same spot on two consecutive days: On day one you may find ten butterflies, and on day two none."

It is impossible to track individual butterflies because of their fragility, the brief life span of some species and difficulty spotting tagged individuals. Tagging experiments in the refuges have been tried in the past with no real success. Tagged butterflies are rarely re-sighted. If an area has unbroken landscape, a tagging program could be helpful; but here on Big Pine, butterflies move through one area into another and are never sighted again. Herein lies the problem: Tagging butterflies just won't work here, and other means of measuring their presence will never reveal their true population, only presence/absence or relative abundance.

Unfortunately, wildlife biologists currently have more questions than answers. However, research is yielding some possible paradigms to account for the dwindling number of Keys butterflies. Some answers are sure to eventuate.

One of the species of butterflies facing assumed extinction, or *extirpation*, is the Florida leafwing, found mostly on Big Pine. These butterflies have not been seen in more than three years. When a species is confined to so small an area, extirpation comes all too easily.

Why worry about butterflies? Most of us would say, because They were here first, or They belong here, or They enhance the quality of life on this island. Less idealistic reasons are also important. The island ecosystem works through symbiosis. Over time, species have become dependent on each other. The propagation of plants depends on butterflies; the nourishment of butterflies depends on those same plants. If one spot in the ecosystem is eliminated, others will be affected as well.

> *"Butterflies are ephemeral species. You can visit the same spot on two consecutive days: On day one you may find ten butterflies, and on day two none."*
> — CHAD ANDERSON

The Butterfly Bush Half Full

Despite the loss of some butterfly populations, others have begun to rebound, thanks to successful wildlife management plans and a good deal of luck. For example, the thumbnail-sized Miami blue butterflies were thought to be extirpated a decade ago, due to Hurricane Andrew, loss of habitat, widespread use of pesticides and other environmental factors. Then, remarkably, a small colony was discovered at Bahia Honda State Park. More recently, a refuge wildlife biologist and a volunteer discovered yet another colony within the boundaries of the Key West National Wildlife Refuge. The outlook is tentative yet promising. Breeding captive butterflies for release has not worked—the released butterflies cannot fend for themselves in the willd—but current management plans seem to be stabilizing the Miami blue populations that already exist.

Despite very legitimate concerns over loss of butterflies, the Keys' refuges continue to serve as a showcase for many species of butterflies: some are permanent residents, others pause here for a rest as they migrate. Almost anywhere you turn within our refuge pinelands, you are likely to spot butterflies.

Endangered Marsh Rabbits

When ocean waters rose enough to create islands, diversity of species became limited. The breeding populations of various species favored those animals best adapted to an island where food and water were in short supply. Therefore, many of the animals in the Key Deer Refuge are smaller than their mainland counterparts, and would be easily eradicated by a single catastrophic event or loss of the last vestiges of their habitat, due to development. Add to this scenario the continuing loss of marshes to the rising ocean, and it is easy to see why the marsh rabbits are critically endangered.

Similar to the diminutive Key deer, Lower Keys marsh rabbits are much smaller than mainland rabbits. They are nocturnal and rarely seen by humans, emerging only at night from the safety of grassy marshes to hunt for food.

Before the arrival of man, rabbits had few natural predators and roamed Big Pine freely. Today, the remaining few marsh rabbits are located north of US 1, trapped in a fragmented habitat, and threatened by a burgeoning population of feral and free-range domestic cats and other predators. There are barriers everywhere, forcing the rabbits into tiny spaces. Housing development has pushed the rabbits close to the edge of extinction. Housing tracts, streets, roads and canals, even mosquito ditches, (shallow ditches lined with concrete and stocked with mosquito larvae-eating fish) make the rabbits easy prey for pursuing cats, large birds and other predators. Others are killed trying to cross the road to safer territory or feeding areas. In the past, hunters killed rabbits regularly, and today a small number of poachers continue to hunt them.

The refuge and a group of concerned residents have been working on a comprehensive plan to save the marsh rabbits. The plan, however, must be graduated over a period of years. An educational program is an important tool: even the publication of this book will aid in that effort. The refuge is

implementing other measures as well. A trapping program for feral cats has been tried in the past with little success. However, the refuge has revamped its predator control program and expects better results. Unfortunately, even if successful, the cats trapped in a spay, neuter and release program will not have a significant impact. Neutered animals can still eat rabbits. This may be the single most difficult problem to solve. Many residents defend the cats' right to live here on Big Pine along with refuge species. The residents feed the feral cats, which does help to keep them well-fed and within a more conscribed area. Others contend that cats do not hunt because they are hungry: they hunt because it is their nature to hunt.

The refuge and civilian stakeholders continue to work toward a mutually acceptable solution. The sad fact, everyone agrees, is that irresponsible pet owners have created this problem. Some allow their domestic cats to roam freely throughout the refuge; others moved away and left their cats behind, or simply abandoned their cats in the refuge when they no longer found it convenient to care for them.

Some suggest that since it is so hard to trap cats, it would be wiser to trap the marsh rabbits and move them to a safer location, establishing new breeding colonies on uninhabited islands. Others suggest putting some of the rabbits in a controlled breeding program. Unfortunately, neither of these ideas is feasible. Marsh rabbits are remarkably hard to trap; they are hard even to find. They rarely leave footprints and do not stay in one spot. Instead, they move around from one patchy marsh to another, making any attempt to trap them a random act. Even if some were to be trapped and transported to another area, they, like the Key deer, would very likely return to their original habitat. Marsh rabbits refuse to breed in captivity, so a captive breeding program is not an answer; and unlike their other rabbit cousins, they breed infrequently, and only two or three babies are born in each litter.

Even a solid count of the marsh rabbits is difficult. Since they are constantly moving and leave few footprints, refuge biologists must look instead for rabbit droppings in various areas of the habitat. Over time, they can compare how many areas are occupied today in comparison to previous years. Thus far, the pattern is discouraging.

Keys Raccoons

Keys raccoons are found in all habitats within the refuge, from hardwood hammocks to pineland meadows, even in marsh and swamp areas. They are omnivorous, dining happily on crabs and insects, fruits and nuts, and just about any other food source on the island. Keys raccoons are adaptable and wily, able to live in almost any terrain, as long as fresh water is present.

You may wonder why raccoons appear in a book about rare and endangered species. You see them all the time, usually at night, and usually hunting for food—sometimes in your garbage can! But Florida Keys raccoons are unique.

Like other refuge species, the breeding colony has been isolated so long in this island chain that they have taken on characteristics and coloring not found anywhere else. Big Pine raccoons differ even from those in Key West or Key Largo. Refuge raccoons are small: Full grown males weigh only six to eight pounds. Their bodies are more streamlined and their fur is much thinner than mainland raccoons; their mask is narrower and their color is lighter. Because this species is distinct from other raccoons, and because one natural catastrophe could eradicate the population, they are guarded by a network of volunteers, despite their stable place in the ecosystem.

Nonprofit wildlife rehabilitators work to ensure both the health and permanence of raccoons within the refuge. They also offer helpful brochures to residents on ways to minimize problems with raccoons.

The two most effective means of discouraging unwelcome raccoons is to take in food and water bowls for house pets each night and to use locking garbage cans or bungee cords to keep raccoons away. If no ready food source is present, most raccoons will move on in search of easier pickings.

Postcards from the Refuge

Birds in the Bush

Any display of Florida postcards includes several featuring flamingos, herons, egrets and other photogenic birds, many living in the Florida Keys. The refuges are the year-round home of so many birds that it is impossible to cover all of them here. In addition, winter winds in northern states tell dozens of northern species to head south. (These are the literal "snowbirds" of south Florida, although the term "snowbirds" now figuratively applies to fortunate people who, like migrating birds, head south to the Keys each fall.) Then consider the many other species that stop in the Keys for an extended respite before continuing their flight even further south. In the spring, as these long range travelers return, it is not unusual for exhausted birds to land on boats at sea because  they just can't fly any longer. Boaters are happy to give the birds a ride to shore, where they can rest before continuing their journey.

This mélange of resident birds, winter birds and migratory birds combine to make the Keys refuges a winter destination for bird watchers, bird watching aficionados and those of us who just like to watch the feathered pageant from our own back yards. It is not surprising, therefore, that the Audubon House is a popular tourist stop in Key West, or that the Florida Keys refuges play a significant role in documenting and understanding the birds who live with us and around us. This same adventure is waiting for you, with or without birding binoculars.

Back From the Brink

Eastern Brown Pelican

The good news concerning the brown pelicans of the Florida Keys is that they seem to be increasing in number, despite some significant setbacks along the way. Fortunately, Keys pelicans were not impacted by the devastating effects of DDT and other pesticides in the decades between 1950 and 1980, when most pelicans in other states were in danger of extirpation. In fact, Florida was instrumental in re-supplying pelicans to Louisiana to establish new nestling colonies after pesticides virtually eliminated pelicans from the area.

However, Keys pelicans have suffered their own misfortunes, due to infestation by parasites, loss of habitat, man's intentional and unintentional interference, and a mysterious illness in 2004 that killed more than 400 wintering birds in the Marquesas Keys. Birds were literally falling, dead, out of the trees, with no prior warning; and even today, the cause of that sudden and virulent illness is still undetermined, despite the best efforts of science to solve the mystery. We do know, however, what was *not* the cause: The birds were not killed by parasites or marine botulism; they were not killed by a red tide. However, the sudden die-off of pelicans coincided with a similar die-off of sea turtles. Were the species impacted by the same deadly presence? That answer, too, is unknown. It does seem possible, although not provable, that the pelicans were infected by pesticides or other contaminants in lakes they visited during their migration to the Marquesas. The troubling result of the die-off, however, is all too clear: We now have only one small colony of nesting brown pelicans between the Seven Mile Bridge and the Marquesas Keys.

> *"The brown pelican symbolizes a species that has come back from the brink of extinction."*
> — TOM WILMERS, REFUGE WILDLIFE BIOLOGIST

How, then, are our marinas, docks and waterways ubiquitously populated by pelicans? How, then, do pelicans follow most commercial fishing boats, scooping up fingerling fish tossed aside when fishing nets are emptied? How is it that pelicans come out of nowhere to beg for fish scraps when the day's catch is being fileted? The answer to these questions may surprise most of us: Those pelicans are merely passing through. They are in the Keys for the same reasons as human tourists: warm, balmy days, a chance to loaf in the sun and the promise of a good fish dinner. Most pelicans belong to nesting colonies elsewhere, and come down to the Keys for some pleasant R & R before returning to their distant homes.

Today, the wildlife agencies here in the Keys have done much to protect brown pelicans. For example, ordinances prohibit the use of pesticides and the dumping of oil and oil derivatives into coastal waters. The horrific photos of oil-soaked pelicans in the spill created by the Deepwater Horizon off the coast of Louisiana, show graphically how deadly oil spills are to pelicans and other water birds. Not only is their ability to dive and capture food compromised, but the oil coats their feathers and prevents them from drying off, creating hypothermia. In addition, when the birds try to groom themselves and remove the oil from their feathers, they ingest oil and very likely will suffer longterm consequences. Here, the work of the Keys wildlife refuges goes beyond ordinances and regulations; in fact, education may be the best tool of the refuges. Partnering with FAVOR, (Friends and Volunteers of Refuges), KPDA, (Key Deer Protection Alliance) and Save-a-Turtle, the refuges are engaged in a multi-faceted program to address some of the most pressing problems threatening wildlife here, including the deadly effects of oil upon wildlife.

> *"When nesting, pelicans are incredibly sensitive to human presence. They nest on the edge of an island, leaving them very vulnerable."*
>
> TOM WILMERS, REFUGE WILDLIFE BIOLOGIST

Because the pelicans nest in mangroves at the outer edges of islands, they are victims of unintentional disturbance from humans. The jarring sound of motorboats and jet skis, for example, frighten the parent birds from the nest, leaving the eggs or newly-hatched babies to overheat in the sun. The shade provided by their parents' bodies is the only safeguard against the sun for young pelicans. The eggs or hatchlings may die after just twenty minutes in the burning sun. Certainly this is an unintended consequence of boaters out for an afternoon of fun. This book and other outreach publications from the refuges will help to inform boaters of this potential danger to baby pelicans.

Another unintentional but nevertheless fatal behavior by boaters and kayakers kills pelicans—or frightens them from the area. Humans love the backcountry for the same reasons the pelicans do: It is a calm and tranquil spot to "get away from it all." Boaters and kayakers go into the edge of the

Postcards from the Refuge

mangroves where pelicans nest. When commercial or recreational sightseeing boats and kayaks draw up close for a better look at the pelicans, they may actually cause the pelicans to flush or, worse, cause them injury. In 1992, the U. S. Fish and Wildlife Service created a countywide management plan that now safeguards specified areas from boaters. Since the refuge owns some of the islands, they can prohibit access to them. As concerned citizens, we can respect rules and safeguards posted in the waters near these islands and encourage others to do so. In general, if you come upon a pelican colony—anywhere—during nesting season, (between mid-March and mid-August), leave immediately. You may save the lives of baby pelicans.

White-Crowned Pigeon

White-crowed pigeons of the Florida Keys are long distance travelers. Although they are considered Florida refuge birds, they migrate between Cuba and other Caribbean islands, to the Florida Keys, where they nest. For this reason, their numbers vary greatly, depending on the season. Nesting occurs roughly between mid-March and mid-August, in the Keys, where food is readily available. During the months when the presence of white-crowned pigeons in the refuge is greatest, sighting them is a treat, if you know where to look. They instinctively choose the most remote locations possible to protect themselves from predators. They nest and eat in two different locations within the Keys, flying as much as thirty miles daily between locations. They nest on mangrove islands in the backcountry and feed on larger Keys, where fruit-bearing trees are plentiful. Much of the recent information on white-crowned pigeons occurred when a young bird suffered a severe laceration, was treated by a local veterinarian, and tagged before release. Refuge personnel were able, then, to observe the same bird over a period of years. Named "Stitches," the pigeon returned each year to the same neighborhood where he had been rescued. Continuing observation of the same pigeon is a rare opportunity.

The species is notable for both its diet and its incredible flying skills. Poisonwood berries comprise most of the white-crowned pigeons' diet, along with various other berries and fruit. The abundance of black torch seeds in nearby Marathon makes that municipality a nucleus for gatherings of white-crowned pigeons, and other species, and a good spot for birdwatchers. The birds are such good flyers that, when strong winds blow, they can fly in any direction to safety, a skill that no doubt enables their movement across vast distances between islands. These birds are an excellent example of the interconnectedness of wildlife within the refuge. Because they eat seeds and berries of trees, they also eliminate seeds through their digestive process, and some of those seeds take root and grow into new trees.

The two greatest threats to the white-crowned pigeon are loss of habitat and hurricanes. Because of the rush to development in the Florida Keys, hardwood hammocks are disappearing beneath bulldozers and the push to build more and more houses in the sunny sub-tropics. Not only do the white-crowned pigeons lose their accustomed habitat, they also lose the

A danger to some, a delicacy to others, poisonwood is a favorite of visiting white crowned pigeons

the poisonwood and other berries that feed them for most of the year. Few homeowners want poisonwood trees, comparable to tree-sized poison ivy, on their property. Although poisonwood is protected, it is slowly disappearing from the area. One important exception is on Key Deer Refuge land and privately owned but undeveloped land on Big Pine. Here, poisonwood continues to be

plentiful; plentiful enough that visitors need to be wary. The droopy leaves and caustic sap of the trees injure even the trees themselves, so humans should avoid touching them altogether.

Hurricanes are the other major threat to the white-crowned pigeon. In recent years, both Hurricane Dennis and Hurricane Wilma devastated the habitat and the white crowned pigeons were, in turn, affected. Fortunately, this species has rebounded recently within our local refuges.

Reddish Egret

Notable as the only wading bird that is entirely coastal, the reddish egret is vulnerable in ways other refuge birds are not. Even though protected now by the Migratory Bird Act, this species has been slow to recoup its numbers. This situation is largely due to human habitation. Humans build homes in the same spots reddish egrets need to nest and feed, so the burgeoning building boom in the Keys is a death knell to reddish egrets. Again, with this species, as with so many others, refuge lands are instrumental in the long-term survival of reddish egrets

Egrets depend on clear, shallow water because they are sight hunters. Wading in four inches of water or less, reddish egrets have a very limited niche of feeding opportunities, dependent entirely upon the tides and the absence of humans and other predators. Largely territorial, the same birds return daily to the same spots to hunt for fish and crustaceans. Sometimes they do an incredible dance to catch their prey, and are not at all methodical in their fishing. They run indiscriminately in all directions and become feisty when challenged or pursued. Refuge workers have difficulty catching and tagging them at any time: Tagging them during mating season is almost impossible. A quiet walk along refuge wetlands may reveal some species of wading birds fishing for a meal; and if you are truly lucky, you may even see one or more reddish egrets. Your chances are greater during non-nesting months, when reddish egrets tend to congregate here.

Although not yet endangered, they very likely will become so. Most possible threats to the survival of this species have come together in the very places that reddish egrets must live. These are not sea grass foragers: They need clean, sheltered lagoons or wetlands for hunting during periods of high winds, and shallow water in order to see prey clearly from above. Highly sensitive to human presence, egrets will not nest in close proximity to human habitation.

As a species, the reddish egret has survived ordeals that would have eliminated most other species. Between the 1890s and the 1930s, reddish egret feathers were greedily harvested for the fashion industry. Women's hats, muffs, and other accessories were made from the birds' gorgeous feathers; but of course the birds died for fashion. Fortunately for reddish egrets, bird feathers have gone out of style, but their numbers continue to plummet. Despite intensive study and tagging of birds, the cause of their decline, other than loss of habitat, has not yet been determined. Tom Wilmers, Refuge Wildlife Biologist, who has studied these remarkable birds for a lifetime, still holds out hope: "They have come through incredible adversity and survived," he says, and he is determined that they will survive this latest challenge as well.

Great White Heron

This gorgeous large white bird, for which the Great White Heron Refuge is named, is sometimes considered the same species as the Great Blue Heron. The Great White is a morph—different in color only—from its blue cousin—and much more rare. The Great White is found only in south Florida, especially the Everglades and the Keys. Its body is bright white with long snowy feathers draping its neck and crest. The bill and the legs are orange. Great Whites are versatile feeders, capable of wading for prey, flying and diving for prey—usually fish—and occasionally coming out of the water to hunt insects and frogs on land. They sometimes stay within a particular area to feed, and become a temporary fixture in the neighborhood.

Turkey Vulture

The turkey vulture plays an important role in the refuge ecosystem. These big, black heavy-bodied birds are masters of efficient flight. They spread their wings and soar on updrafts and thermals, rarely flapping their wings. At night, they sleep in tall trees or on roofs with other turkey vultures. A roof covered with turkey vultures is a spectacle worthy of Edgar Allan Poe! During the day, they search for and eat dead animals or carrion. Almost anywhere in the Keys, groups of these birds can be seen circling their next meal or covering most of a tree, sitting and waiting their turn to eat. The heads have no feathers and are dull red like a turkey—thus the name "turkey" vulture. As parents, they are not particular about their nests: They nest almost anywhere, including hollow limbs on trees, deserted buildings, even on the ground. Despite the large number of turkey vultures present in the refuges during winter, most are migratory and will head north at the end of the season, leaving only a small colony of turkey vultures to live here permanently.

The refuges of the Florida Keys provide appealing habitats for scores of birds, both endemic, or year-round species, and migratory birds. In winter, the refuge is resplendent with gorgeous birds, large and small: some with such sweet songs you wish they would sing all day, some with harsh cries, grunts and shrieks, and one with the purring sound of a cat. The lower humidity and cooler temperatures make any walk in the refuge a special occasion. The Blue Hole and the Watson-Mannillo nature trails are well-marked and wheel chair accessible. For those visitors who prefer an off-the-trail adventure, the fire roads throughout the refuge are open to hikers. They go so deep into the brush that few people follow them very far. (Just stay on the narrow dirt road, and you won't get lost.) Although marked, "Unauthorized Entry Prohibited", the fire roads are open for hiking but not vehicles. Only the areas marked "Area Closed" are off-limits. These sections of the refuge are set aside for deer and other species to live naturally, without the presence of humans. Be sure to take your camera along on your walk; you never know what you will see! There are always abundant opportunities for both amateur and professional photographers to snap memorable photos of birds: your own personal Postcards from the Refuge.

These are just a small sampling of the birds that share their habitat with us. There are numerous books and references for the avid bird watcher, The refuge visitor center can provide printed materials and even suggest spots where you might see various species.

Great white heron

Baby green heron

Eastern kingbird

Crested fly catcher

Indigo bunting

Great blue heron

Osprey

Postcards from the Refuge

Protecting The Refuge

Invasive Exotics: Intruders in Paradise

Postcards from the Refuge

Intruders in Paradise

Invasive Predators

For a very long time, the ecosystem in the Keys was balanced. The endemic species had adapted to the environment, and there were virtually no threats to that balance. Then man arrived, and the balance of species become ever more precarious until, now, some species have already been extirpated, and others face the same fate. Not only was man himself a threat, through an increasing loss of habitat for wildlife; but he also imported various commodities to make his life here more comfortable. Along with those commodities came unseen predators that would change the ecosystem forever.

Flora

Many invasive species traveled to the Keys unnoticed, as unseen cargo on trees, fruits and vegetables that were intended to make man's existence on this isolated network of Keys more attractive. For example, it is widely believed that Australian pines were seeded by man throughout the Keys, with the idea that their root systems would prevent erosion. However, the ironic and unforeseen result was that those areas would become monocultural, with ensuing beach erosion. In other words, Australian pines forced out other plants—such as sea oats—that are necessary for the preservation of existing beaches. In addition, pine needles drop to the ground and form an acidic mat that chokes out native plants. This is true throughout the refuge, not only on beaches and marshes. Birds and wind carry seeds with them, and drop them haphazardly. Thus, the balance of nature is distorted and repercussions are felt throughout the ecosystem.

Young Australian pines tower over native trees

Brazilian pepper, also known as Florida holly, *(opposite page)* another invasive species, was imported by landscapers. The trees' bright red berries and dark green leaves created a brilliant contrast to the lesser greens of endemic plants. However, they soon became a nightmare for the refuge and homeowners alike. The red berries are plenteous and easily transmitted to other locations by birds, small animals, and warm tropical breezes. Other berries fall to the ground and create a thorny nest of new Brazilian peppers around the parent plant. With due vigilance, homeowners can kill and dig out the undesirable progeny. On refuge land, however, the problem is greatly magnified. Unlike the homeowner, no one can comb the hundreds of acres of refuge land for unwanted seedlings. Even many landowners fight a continual battle against this pervasive intruder. Their land may be located alongside an unmaintained lot owned by a distant landlord, and the proliferation of Brazilian peppers is made more complicated. Neither the neighbor nor the refuge has the legal right to cull out undesirable plants and seedlings from someone else's property.

Another perplexing problem is that large Brazilian pepper trees do not burn. Therefore, they cannot be eradicated by prescribed fires. Brazilian peppers change the entire behavior of the fire. Only small saplings burn, while the older trees remain intact, to continue spreading their seeds throughout the refuge, and displacing indigenous species.

Fortunately, the refuge here has been awarded state grants and "in-kind" incentives to aid in the fight against Brazilian peppers and Australian pines. Each year, tech crews with natural science backgrounds comb through Big Pine and other areas of the refuge, eradicating the encroachment of Brazilian peppers and Australian pines. They even extend their service to property owners who request it through the refuge. This program has been very successful, and is considered a model for other wildlife refuges facing similar problems.

> *"We've done what we can about human encroachment and habitat loss. Now we must ensure that the ecosystem functions as naturally as possible."*
> — CHAD ANDERSON, REFUGE BIOLOGIST

Fauna

Beyond invasive flora, the refuge is besieged by invasive fauna, which present other threats. Perhaps the most readily noticeable is the burgeoning presence of iguanas. While these large and flamboyant lizards are popular with visitors to the area, their presence in the refuge has changed the ecosystem. Some of these invaders may have arrived on Big Pine as a side effect of hurricanes from Cuba, while others, perhaps most, are the progeny of pets released by irresponsible owners. To be fair, some professionals are hoping to prove that iguanas are indigenous to Big Pine. However, their effort at this time is incomplete, and refuge staff, who have been here over the decades, recall no iguanas until the mid 1990s.

Some iguanas are meat-eaters, but most here in the refuge are vegetarians. While on the surface, they may seem to pose no danger to endemic species, the iguanas eat not only flowers and plants, but also species living on the plants. For example, they eat tree snails along with foliage, and dine on flowers that endemic species need for food. There are few enough flowering plants, and those that we do have growing in the wild, have traditionally been eaten by Key deer. Wild-growing butterfly orchids are threatened because iguanas eat the flowers, preventing the orchids from seeding new plants. The nearly extirpated Miami Blue butterfly traditionally lays its eggs on knicker bean plants. The eggs hatch into larvae that normally would live on the plants' branches; but iguanas eat the knicker beans, and along with the beans, they consume the butterfly larvae as well.

Although most iguanas spotted in residential neighborhoods are pet-store size, they grow another four to five feet, if left undisturbed in the woods. Imagine how much food is required each day to feed an iguana of that size! Then multiply that by the number of large iguanas within the refuge, and you begin to see the enormity of the problem.

Fire ants are nobody's friends. They are aggressive and attack—in hordes—nearly anything that disturbs their mounds. Immediately following fire ant bites, humans feel fiery welts beginning to form on the skin. Thus the name 'fire ants'. Stock Island tree snails fare even worse: Fire ants seek them out and eat them. These snails are currently facing extirpation. It is interesting to note that fire ants are not native to the Keys. Like many other invasive species, they rode in on produce trucks or flotsam "rafts" from the mainland or other islands, and spread rapidly through the Keys. You might even say they spread like wildfire.

No one can spend much time in the refuge without seeing one or more little lizards. While seeming to be iconic of the Keys, most of the lizards are not native. Not as visible as their iguana cousins, they are far more prevalent, almost overwhelming in their numbers. Cuban or brown anoles feed on insects living on native plants. Even worse, they eat butterfly larvae along the leaves that harbor them. Geckos also came into the refuge, and have become invasive here. Much larger than anoles, geckos are popular photos for visitors.

Even those cute tree frogs are interlopers. Unintentionally introduced into the refuge on potted plants or as released pets, these invasive frogs have pushed aside native tree frogs and blanketed the refuge with their offspring. According to the Florida Fish and Wildlife Commission, a single female Cuban tree frog can lay 4,000 eggs at one time, three times more than the native green tree frog. They feast on native species, including endemic tree frogs. Further, Cuban tree frogs and marine toads secrete a toxin that can sicken or kill domestic pets and wildlife.

> *"It all comes down to the same thing: irresponsible pet owners."*
>
> ALISON HIGGINS, OUR ANIMAL FAMILY

Some exotic species do not themselves attack or eat endemic plants or animals, but nevertheless pose hidden threats to wildlife. Yet, their existence in the refuge may upset the balance of species.

Invasive Snakes

Recently, dangerous exotic, or non-native, snakes have escaped or been released into the Everglades and the Florida Keys. They are a dangerous threat to most native species, including humans. The Nature Conservancy and USFWS have undertaken the serious business of eliminating them before they do irreparable damage. These large and aggressive snakes threaten the existence of struggling species of mammals, amphibians and reptiles.

The sad truth is that these invaders were originally introduced into the Keys' fragile ecosystem by human pet owners. No doubt, most of the irresponsible pet owners had no idea of the harm their pets would pose to wildlife, but the threat becomes more dire every day.

The news media has concentrated on the Burmese python, probably because their numbers in the wild are most alarming. Originally, these constrictor snakes were purchased through pet shops, where the six to eight inch baby pythons seemed to be intriguing pets. They cost only $50.00, and could live comfortably in a small cage or aquarium. Feeding the python and cleaning the cage was easy. At first, that is. But the Burmese pythons grew fast, required larger and larger cages, and meals higher on the food chain. No one wants to feed live rabbits or rats to a six foot python. The care of such snakes soon became dangerous and next to impossible. An easy answer seemed to be the release of oversized pythons into the vastness of the Everglades or a wildlife refuge. Unfortunately, Burmese pythons cover a large range and breed easily, with an average of eighty eggs per clutch, and live for twenty-five to thirty years. Also, they are remarkably adept at finding one another. Adults reach a length of twelve feet or more and are a threat to any species smaller than they are—including humans. Especially children. Eliminating, or at least drastically reducing the presence of pythons, is an important goal for the refuges. At this time, sightings of pythons have been rare in the Keys, and wildlife specialists are working to keep it that way.

Equally dangerous are boa constrictors, which also are beginning to appear in the Keys. At this writing, there is a boa constrictor on a neighboring Key. It is estimated to be eleven feet long and twenty inches in circumference, and has been there for five years. Wildlife biologists have verified its presence but have not yet been able to capture it. In addition, an officer of Key Deer Refuge law enforcement recently caught and killed a six-foot-long boa constrictor; three days earlier he had sighted another one but had been unable to capture it.

Fortunately, the future is not grim. Constrictor snakes in the wild will be challenged, thanks to the python patrol recently formed by the Nature Conservancy and USFWS. In addition, an amnesty day is held each year by Fish and Wildlife in conjunction with Miami Metro Zoo. Owners of dangerous pets can take them to the zoo and hand them over with no questions asked. The zoo places them in zoos and other appropriate venues. This program is popular with pet owners who initially did not understand how large their pets could become or how much danger they could pose. This amnesty program includes all exotic pets, not only constrictor snakes.

Any sighting of a constrictor snake should be reported immediately to the refuge or the Florida Fish and Wildlife Commission.

Defending
The Refuge

Volunteers Matter
How You Can Help
Afterword

Postcards from the Refuge

Volunteers Matter

The Lower Keys appeal to those who love nature and enjoy life in a rural setting. Likewise, many of the residents are passionate about preservation of refuge land and animal rights. It is hard to imagine a single site where volunteer work is more needed or more appreciated. The National Key Deer Refuge provides crucial habitat to many threatened and endangered species, and the work is endless. The refuge personnel rely upon volunteers at the office, the visitor center, the Blue Hole, the nature trails and other spots within the refuge. In fact, volunteers were already working with the refuge before any formal volunteer organizations were established.

Refuge volunteers work tirelessly. They help maintain trails and signage, and position buoys around outer islands of the refuge to prohibit motorized boat traffic and other intrusions into the natural life of birds. On Big Pine and other Key deer habitats, volunteers remove invasive, exotic plants, which, when allowed to dominate the landscape, radically change the ecosystem and negatively impact the plants and animals within it. The deer have survived for hundreds of years on native plants: If those food sources are crowded out, the health of the herd will be affected. As the dominant species in the refuge, any adversity for the deer filters down to all the other species. In effect, ensuring the health of the deer ensures the health of other species as well. Refuge volunteers function as genial sentinels guarding the welfare of the refuge.

The Key Deer Protection Alliance, KDPA, as its name indicates, is a local organization that focuses on the Key deer and keeps a sharp eye on policies that may affect the deer. They also have annual scholarship awards, various projects that benefit the Key deer, and are the legal support when fighting for the Key deer means lending a legal helping hand.

FAVOR, Friends And Volunteers Of Refuges - Florida Keys, is another very active local group. FAVOR not only raises money through their Key Deer Bookstore & Gift Shop and fund-raising events, it also promotes and funds educational projects and community awareness activities. Besides staffing the bookstore and visitor center, FAVOR volunteers lead educational nature walks, kayaking tours and many other programs to help people learn more about the refuge.

Often, individual members see something that needs doing—and do it—without fanfare or publicity. The volunteers say the camaraderie and their sense of purpose are the only rewards they need.

How You Can Help

Both locals and visitors can help the refuge.

Locals can:

Join an early morning beach clean up
- Volunteer at the Blue Hole
- Volunteer at the visitor center and bookstore
- Help to maintain trails and outer islands
- Help to disseminate information about campaigns to aid the refuge
  - A recent example is Give a Smidgen for the White Crowned Pigeon, which encourages residents to restore native trees and shrubs as food sources for white crowned pigeons and other species
- Join FAVOR and/or KDPA

Visitors can:
- Join a guided nature walk or kayak trip to learn about the refuge
- Support legislation to benefit wildlife refuges nation-wide
- Use cloth bags instead of single use plastic when shopping. Plastic can be lethal to animals
- Recycle, at home and away from home
- Pick up trash, even if it's not yours
- Reduce or eliminate your use of pesticides, fertilizer and other substances harmful to the ocean, canals and wildlife
- Help to teach others that human actions can impact wildlife

Afterword

The Florida Keys is an inspirational place for writers, photographers and scientists. In fact, we were inspired to learn more about *everything*; but not being scientists ourselves, we first checked in with our friends and neighbors. We were intrigued to learn just how many experts we have living here. The result, *Postcards From the Refuge, a Journey Through the National Key Deer Refuge*, is just that, a postcard or snapshot of what you find when you visit the refuge. There are many excellent books and publications written by guides, biologists, botanists and historians available for you to further your own education in the areas that most intrigue you, and most are available at the refuges' Visitor Center and the Key Deer Bookstore.

Photo Credits

Our heartfelt thanks go to those who graciously allowed us to use their photos in this book.

U.S. Fish & Wildlife Service, National Key Deer Refuge Archives, pages 20, 22, 27, 37, 40, 41, 45, 46, 49, 50, 53, 57, 65

Reproduced courtesy of the "Ding" Darling Wildlife Society, page 21

Mickey Foster, page 57

Michelle Wisniewski, pages 42, 47, 52, 54, 57

Alyssa Johnson, page 63

All other photos, graphics, and drawings by Nancy Chatelaine

Postcards from the Refuge

Made in the USA
Las Vegas, NV
03 August 2021